Between Intellect & Instinct

DEMYSTIFYING

the OFFICE of the PROPHET

Between Intellect & Instinct

DEMYSTIFYING

---

the OFFICE of the PROPHET

Sharon Luzzi

Copyright

Copyright © 2015 by **Sharon Luzzi**. All rights reserved. This book or any portion thereof may not be reproduced or used in any manner whatsoever without the express written permission of **Sharon Luzzi** except for the use of brief quotations in a book review.

Printed in the United States of America

First Printing, 2015

ISBN-13: 978-1-942022-22-0
ISBN-10: 1942022220

The Butterfly Typeface Publishing
PO BOX 56193
Little Rock Arkansas 72215

Dedication

*This book is dedicated to
Yeshua Ha Mashiach,
the Kingdom of God
and the
Millennial Reign.*

The Future Glory of Israel

Isaiah Chapter 60

1Arise, shine, for your light has come, and the glory of the Lord has risen upon you.

2For behold, darkness shall cover the earth, and thick darkness the peoples; but the Lord will arise upon you, and his glory will be seen upon you.

3And nations shall come to your light, and kings to the brightness of your rising.

4Lift up your eyes all around, and see; they all gather together, they come to you; your sons shall come from afar, and your daughters shall be carried on the hip.

5Then you shall see and be radiant; your heart shall thrill and exult, because the abundance of the sea shall be turned to you, the wealth of the nations shall come to you.

6A multitude of camels shall cover you, the young camels of Midian and Ephah; all those from Sheba shall come. They shall bring gold and frankincense, and shall bring good news, the praises of the Lord.

7All the flocks of Kedar shall be gathered to you; the rams of Nebaioth shall minister to you; they shall come up with acceptance on my altar, and I will beautify my beautiful house.

8 Who are these that fly like a cloud, and like doves to their windows?

9 For the coastlands shall hope for me, the ships of Tarshish first, to bring your children from afar, their silver and gold with them, for the name of the Lord your God, and for the Holy One of Israel, because he has made you beautiful.

10 Foreigners shall build up your walls, and their kings shall minister to you; for in my wrath I struck you, but in my favor I have had mercy on you.

11 Your gates shall be open continually; day and night they shall not be shut, that people may bring to you the wealth of the nations, with their kings led in procession.

12 For the nation and kingdom that will not serve you shall perish; those nations shall be utterly laid waste.

13 The glory of Lebanon shall come to you, the cypress, the plane, and the pine, to beautify the place of my sanctuary, and I will make the place of my feet glorious.

14 The sons of those who afflicted you shall come bending low to you, and all who despised you shall bow down at your feet; they shall call you the City of the Lord, the Zion of the Holy One of Israel.

15 Whereas you have been forsaken and hated, with no one passing through, I will make you majestic forever, a joy from age to age.

16You shall suck the milk of nations; you shall nurse at the breast of kings; and you shall know that I, the Lord, am your Savior and your Redeemer, the Mighty One of Jacob.

17Instead of bronze I will bring gold, and instead of iron I will bring silver; instead of wood, bronze, instead of stones, iron. I will make your overseers peace and your taskmasters' righteousness.

18Violence shall no more be heard in your land, devastation or destruction within your borders; you shall call your walls Salvation, and your gates Praise.

19The sun shall be no more your light by day, nor for brightness shall the moon give you light; but the Lord will be your everlasting light, and your God will be your glory.

20Your sun shall no more go down, nor your moon withdraw itself; for the Lord will be your everlasting light, and your days of mourning shall be ended.

21Your people shall all be righteous; they shall possess the land forever, the branch of my planting, the work of my hands, that I might be glorified.

22The least one shall become a clan, and the smallest one a mighty nation; I am the Lord; in its time I will hasten it.

"Wherefore thus saith the Lord God of hosts, Because ye speak this word, behold, I will make my words in thy mouth fire, and this people wood, and it shall devour them."

Jeremiah 5:14

Table Of Contents

Introduction

Chapter 1: Who are these people anyway? (P. 22)

Chapter 2: The early life (P. 28)

Chapter 3: Growing pains (P. 36)

Chapter 4: The mature Prophet (P. 50)

Chapter 5: Attributes of the office of the Prophet (P.58)

Chapter 6: The Prophet's spiritual condition (P. 70)

Chapter 7: The role of the office of the Prophet (P. 74)

Chapter 8: Authority (P. 78)

Chapter 9: Rebellion against authority (P. 84)

Chapter Ten: The heart of God (P. 89)

Conclusion

Foreword

On a more personal level I would like to say that in my walk with God, I always had in my spirit, that things were not as they should be. My thoughts bordered on "Am I crazy?" to "We have walked so far away from God and we do not even know how far we have gone." As a young person growing up in a very dead religious church, I knew things were very askew.

Every time I attended another Sunday service I would actually get physically ill. On the major church Holidays I always seemed to be depressed and sick with something.

I of course had to attend with my parents and siblings, but really I felt dead.

As a younger child, I seemed to have wisdom beyond my years and this was even noticed by my peers and so I learned to keep my mouth shut. I started having dreams that came to pass. I had visions and other supernatural experiences. I often got into trouble for my direct truth.

As the years passed God became real and at the age of 25 I was done with organized religion. I sat in a pew and asked God, "Who are you?" He then explained what He wanted me to know and how to pursue Him. *I will be putting that in a later book.*

He kept me on a very exciting path to revealing Himself and how He REALLY IS.

I hope this book is the beginning of sharing to the world who HE REALLY IS.

I was face down in a church service one day and was complaining to God what was going on in the community of believers I was with. He gently responded to my bad attitude with, "I have been misrepresented." So in His loving way He acknowledged what I knew deep down in my heart. He made sure He validated what I was seeing and gently taught me how to see it the way He does.

I will also say that I did not want to share my relationship with God or what I had learned about him in a real way with other people. He told me I needed to in order to bring true liberty to others. This book is the public sharing of what I learned and for the benefit of others.

It is only the beginning.

I pray for pure truth for each and every one who seeks the Living God, the God of Abraham, Isaac and Jacob.

Special Acknowledgment

A special thank you to Jo Ann Velasco.

Without your contribution,

this book would not have been published.

Acknowledgments

I am super happy to write this book!

Although, I need to thank from the depths of my heart, the following people:

All three of my children, whom I love dearly. I am sure you realize by now you lived in somewhat of a fishbowl at times.

To Laura and Van for being a set of parents I needed and were God-breathed.

To all of my Warrior Sisters: Deedee, Carla, Kim, Red, Ruth Ann, Kathy, Donna, Esther, Jael, Debbie and Jo Ann. Without you I would have never made it through. The greatest unsung heroes in my life. The late night phone calls, prayers and tears.

I am grateful for every person sent alongside of me to help me along this journey.

Introduction

The Office of the Prophet is a highly misunderstood and misrepresented function in the body of believers. The Prophet's job is never fully realized until there is the true need for the Office.

The Prophet's job aligns with the government of God himself. The Prophet does not align himself with man or manmade rules and agendas. (We are not talking about disobeying civil laws of the land unless they are crossing over God's laws.) The government of God is most often brushed aside and not believed. *Yeshua* came to save us from the punishment from sin and teach us how to walk out the whole word of God in Love. We have lost sight of being aligned with the true government of God.

The Prophet is usually not wanted, welcomed or received by a large majority of people. You would never recognize one until they come into their fullness. They are as a person, ignored, most often ridiculed and not seen as important to anyone. More importantly, they will never tell you they are a Prophet.

Chapter One

Who are these people anyway?

Their Saga

Prophets are spiritually war torn and not understandable because they are spiritually advanced a good 50 years ahead of the general population of believers. Quite honestly no one is on the same plane of conversation with them for understanding their relationship with God.

The experiences are not the same as others therefore they often have no one to relate to or with. In their growing process they often outgrow friends and tend to look isolated from others. The relationship they have with God even appears to others as they have an exclusive relationship with God. It may seem like others need not apply to the relationship they have with God.

Prophets do not look right, dress funny, are stand offish and often are quiet. Even though they are the mouth piece for God, they wait for the appointed times to speak. They are mocked, glossed over, ignored and placated. God has to be the strength to hold them together to help them to continue on.

The other dilemmas they often face are the following:

Cut off by people from needed resources for their development (which God always has a way around), walked over, looked over, trampled on, betrayed, gone around, starved out, shouted out, abused, used, misused, parlayed, relayed, portrayed, navigated, pushed over the top of, minced, diced, sliced, dried out, burnt, cried out, boiled and steamed.

The usage of all of the above mentioned scenarios will bring the Prophet to his *personal* death. The death of all of themselves. They have willingly gone through the process of this to be used for the perfect will of God. The pain they experience is often excruciating that applies to all areas of their life.

When they go through this *baptism of fire* they can truly speak out the heart of God.

Their entire life revolves around God and seems extreme to fellow believers. The object of their dying to self is to represent God properly. God has been misrepresented for a very long time and we will now start to see the course correction for the foundation of God's government.

After the death of a Prophet, then they are sought after, honored, adored, and lifted into the spotlight. They are brought into remembrance, resurrected, glorified and hoped to be heard from. They are then graced, held up to be an example and used for wisdom.

But isn't it too late? After all they are dead.

Imagine the leader of over a million people in a desert being your responsibility. What will you do with them? God is the one you are responsible to. Could YOU do it? Can you even imagine?

Being a Prophet is an enduring and humble job. No glamour, no glitz.

You can't fake the attributes of a Prophet, let alone wish it into existence. The Prophet is far from being the center of attention for the body of believers.

They are the unsung heroes every day, at all times, in every place of their life here on Earth. They know the value and extent of God and His Kingdom. God has center stage, no one or nothing else.

The stage is set and Moses has to contend with the Pharaoh's of the land. What will he do? He will consult with God first and no one or nothing else.

God is a very essential part of their being. They do not find anything else an option. The Prophet doesn't know any other way to get the information they need to get the job done. God is their only trusted source. The connection between God and the Prophet is undeniable and unbroken.

The Prophet cannot rely on anyone or anything else knowing the results would be disastrous. They know the source is the perfect solution and the only way it can work. Relying on the perfect will of God is the only solution. The plan of God translates into the perfect will of God for the people.

The Prophet executes the will of God. This gives the people the path or direction for where God is needing them to be.

Coming out of Egypt was a massive undertaking for Moses and for the people he led out. Moses had to deal with plagues, magicians, astrologers, more plagues, Pharaoh, booty and the people he was leading.

Moses had to have people skills under pressure of being captured himself and becoming an indentured slave. Moses had to believe what God told him to say and in the results of what he said. Moses had to believe that God's people would be released. Moses couldn't be moved by the fact that Pharaoh would make the children of Israel's jobs harder to the point of death. Moses had to have a heart to withstand the pressure that Pharaoh put on the people. He was in need of being consoled by God.

The Prophet has no idea about what is ahead of them in many ways even though they hear God clearly and have a general idea of what is on the heart of God at any given time. They are required to be obedient to that instruction and move forward with what God has told them. They know that the instruction carries them far out into the future to what they need to know and what is coming.

The faith level of the Prophet hearing, believing and carrying out what is given to him is of epic proportions. He will not be able to move forward with the will of God unless he believes. That is why his heart is fully tested and healed to carry out the task at hand. The task at hand may be as simple as picking up a piece of paper discarded on the ground or it may be parting the Red Sea. It is all about the obedience not the trouble!

Faith is the undergirding of the Prophet's whole life. It is the doorway to accomplishing the will of God. The Hebrew word for faith is transliterated from **aman** (Strong's primitive root word **H539**) meaning the following: trustworthy, support confirm, uphold, established made firm, sure, lasting, verified, to be certain, and nourish.

These are deposited into the Prophet to move in the will and promise of God.

The workings during the life of the Prophet to instill the level of faith required to carry out the task are many and varied. These processes are built on layers of real life. Nowhere else can this be done except through personal experience. Depending on how God created that person for the job is how it will be worked into that Prophet's life.

Chapter Two

Early Life

The Growing Young Prophet

Prophets of God, do not choose the lifestyle they come up in. Nor do they have the ability to change it. The course that God has fixed for them is fixed in them. God so chooses to hide them in a concealed/revealed manner. No one can guess who they are because they have been hidden. Often their families do not even know. They are born into complete obscurity.

Being born into obscurity affords God himself to train and groom this chosen person.

The obscurity is a form of protection for the Prophet. It keeps other people from interfering with the process that God had purposed and planned. Many Prophets will suffer abuse during these early years. The Prophet as a child will be kept aside even in a family, in the form of, the only gender and other things that keep them aside such as socio-economic and geographic culture. The hiding is in a specific family, generation, nationality, community, church denomination, city, country. Last and not least, time frame.

The child doesn't need to be in the perfect family, church denomination, surroundings or pedigree. The current culture and place in time is very important for the Prophet's understanding to what will eventually be known to the Prophet as their target group.

Their childhood up to early adult give discipline and keen identification of things ahead. As a child they know something is different. They have unusual and great times of wisdom they do not know how they received. Discernment is present at an early age which often gets them into trouble with their elders. It can often come in the form of speaking truth abruptly. The innate sense of knowing things guides them on their path with little or no training from anyone else. The strangeness that starts as a child lasts into adulthood. The *strangeness* that I am speaking about is usually the perception of those around them. Even at a young age they have no fear. They acquire sense of navigating life at a high level of perception and sensitivity to their path like no one else. They appear to be stubborn to others but refuse to "go along" with what others think, feel and try to will them to do other than what God has put in them. God has secured his DNA in them for success. The depth that God puts in them spills out around them and is often shunned and looked down upon and downright hated. God has his very hand on them to secure their destiny and the fullness of who he created them to be.

As the young Prophet grows in years, the bumps along the way are many and quite painful. The *bumps* include not understanding why they don't do anything "right."

The truth is that often they are being opposed no matter what they do.

Right or wrong do not even enter into the picture. The very spirit of God that is within them is offensive to all that they come in contact with. They are never part of any crowd.

Because of the many bumps they become alone. To the outside world they are considered aloof, a snob, stuck up, a loner, a non-conformist, out of the loop, not popular, strange, ambiguous, unapproachable, too conservative, religious, and every adjective contrary to who they really are. They are never received or ever understood.

They are scorned, laughed at, insulted, shunned, ignored, put off, attacked, targeted and purposely ridiculed. They are never popular and no ever knows their name. No one would ever suspect who they really are. All of the bumps along with any other factors forms them for the call. It can't be done any other way. All of the shaping molding, firing, and refining is done in the way of their prescribed life. The hand of God forms them nothing else.

Let's take Moses' life as an example. I am going to set the stage before Moses' birth starting in **Exodus chapter 1:1** thru **Exodus chapter 1:22** (St. Jerome Edition)

The sons of Jacob who went to Egypt with him, each with his family, were Reuben, Simeon, Levi, Judah, Issachar, Zebulun Benjamin, Dan, Naphtali,

Gad, and Asher. The total number of these people directly descended from Jacob was seventy. His son Joseph was already in Egypt. In the course of time Joseph, his brothers, and all the rest of that generation died, but their descendants the Israelites, had many children and became so numerous and strong that Egypt was filled with them.

Then a new king, who knew nothing about Joseph, came to power in Egypt. He said to his people, "These Israelites are so numerous and strong that they are a threat to us. In case of war they might join our enemies in order to fight against us, and escape from the country. We must find some way to keep them from becoming even more numerous." So the Egyptians put slave drivers over them to crush their spirits with hard labor. The Israelites built the cities of Pithom and Rameses to serve as supply centers for the king. But the more the Egyptians oppressed the Israelites, the more they increased in number and farther they spread throughout the land. The Egyptians came to fear the Israelites and made their lives miserable by forcing them into cruel slavery.

They made them work on their building projects and in their fields, and they had no pity on them. Then the king of Egypt spoke to Shiphah and Puah, the two midwives who helped the Hebrew women. "When you help the Hebrew women give birth," he said to them, "Kill the baby if it is a boy; but if it is a girl, let it live." But the midwives were God-fearing and so did not obey the king; instead, they let the boys live. So the king sent for the midwives and asked them, "Why are you doing this? Why are you letting the boys live?" They answered, "The Hebrew women are not like Egyptian women; they give birth easily, and their babies are born before either of us gets there."

Because the midwives were God-fearing, God was good to them and gave then families of their own. And the Israelites continued to increase and become strong.

Finally the king issued a command to all his people:

"Take every newborn Hebrew boy and throw him into the Nile, but let all the girls live."

Moses was born at a time where human life had no worth. Today abortion is just a form of birth control without consideration for human life. The king's purpose was to do away with a threat to a human throne. The life of a human being that was in opposition to his way of thinking. This picture existed when *Yeshua* the Messiah was discovered and the king of the day wanted every child two years and under to be destroyed. Why? *Yeshua's* birth was a threat to a human throne.

The Egyptians also were only interested in furthering their kingdom at the expense of God's people. Moses was being born into a time of cruelty to God's people. As we read above they were slaves to an Egyptian king and kingdom.

Let us continue with **Exodus Chapter 2:1 through Exodus Chapter 2:10** (St. Jerome Edition), the birth of Moses.

During this time a man from the tribe of Levi married a woman of his own tribe, and she bore him a son. When she saw what a fine baby he was, she hid him for three months.

But when she could not hide him any longer, she took a basket of reeds and covered it with tar to make it watertight. She put the baby in it and then placed it in the tall grass at the edge of the river. The baby's sister stood some distance away to see what would happen to him. The king's daughter came down to the river to bathe, while her servants walked along the bank. Suddenly she noticed the basket in the tall grass and sent a slave girl to get it. The princess opened it and saw a baby boy. He was crying and she felt sorry for him. "This is one of the Hebrew babies," she said.

Then his sister asked her, "Shall I go and call a Hebrew woman to nurse the baby for you?"

"Please do" she answered. So the girl went and brought the baby's own mother. The princess told the woman, "Take this baby and nurse him for me, and I will pay you." So she took the baby and nursed him. Later, when the child was old enough, she took him to the king's daughter, who adopted him as her own son. She said to herself, "I pulled him out of the water, and so I name him Moses."

Moses' life was not the warm cozy family life you would have expected. He was born during a time of strife in a kingdom where your gender automatically warranted death.

He was separated almost immediately from his parents, floated down a river and given to another family.

We know the story continues with God intervening in his infinite wisdom and protection for his people. He reaches the heart of a servant girl to rescue Moses out of a watery death and places him in the care of a compassionate princess for the rest of his life as a child. This action allows Moses to learn the culture that he would later need to know intimately for his dealing with Pharaoh and the Egyptians.

This reference to Moses gives us a huge insight of how God places his servants in regular everyday life. Prophets lives are well hidden in the mundane daily activities of life while God is using those activities to train the Prophet. It can never be underestimated how God chooses and places his Prophets in the midst of obscurity.

Chapter Three

Growing Pains

Overcoming the Ways of Man

The greatest internal struggle for the Prophet is to enter the heart of God. The Prophet takes the heart of God to the people for their salvation. When the Prophet enters the heart of God, he is learning how to reveal God himself to the people. Thus this is how the Prophet becomes the mouthpiece for God.

The internal struggle is a constant ongoing struggle until brought to perfection to be released to the people. The internal struggle is formed by the external suffering, driving the Prophet deeper and deeper into the heart of God. Learning the ways of God and the love of God. This is all to point the people back to the true ways of God. Hence the heart of God for his people. A personal knowing of God for the purpose of the people accepting God and redemption for their life.

As the growing pains continue, the steps of maturing into the Prophet become a detailed script in the hand of God. It forms all that needs to be formed in the Prophet's heart.

The formation includes:

faithfulness, determination, courage, discipline, personal knowledge of God and his ways, intimacy, character, the image of God, gifts of the Spirit, fruit of the Spirit, and love.

It is often accomplished through reading the word, all kinds of tests and trials, and constant submission of their heart to God. Receiving deliverance, healing and desires to imitate *Yeshua*.

The Prophet carries the heart of God and this is how he accomplishes his task.

The formation of these attributes help the Prophet with a specific set of job duties.

This set of job duties are now an outward sign of what has been going on inside the heart of the Prophet.

This has usually gone on for a prolonged amount of time. It is never an easy process or an alternate process.

They are as follows:

- He or she will speak the heart of God for many different reasons
- Learn how to be an intercessor to the extent of a warrior on the battlefield
- Participates in Judgement
- Cares about societal ills and has a part in addressing those issues

- Reinforces the ways of God
- Develops the ways of God in other people
- A Watchman
- Knows the sign of the times
- Takes an axe to the faulty foundations
- Takes care of the poor and widows
- Takes the Land
- Establishes the Government of God
- Points the children's hearts back to their Fathers

The above list is a general picture of the Prophet's job duties.

The Prophet's job duties will include the people group they will speak to (a specific nation) and depending on what is needed to that specific people group the Prophet will be properly equipped to do that.

They may be multicultural or only geared for one type of people group. Again the Prophet may have had speech and debate classes coupled with the *Ruach Hakodesh* (Holy Spirit) to present the information. Grooming by God's hand. Detailed in such a way that it is undeniable that God did the work in that Prophet's heart.

God gives each Prophet the personality and the understanding for each assignment.

God has them mixed in every culture, geographical location, household, and all the aforementioned places they are hidden in until the time of revealing and need.

The following are encouraging words for those being formed and in need of healing ...

HIS GREAT LOVE

To the Fatherless Generation
Who I have My Mighty Hand on,

Your place in History is a great one.

I had to have a Fatherless generation
To put my imprint on.

My character, My love, My very proof of My love.

A chosen Generation to bring My Love on the earth
A Generation without the imprint of a human father.
So I could breathe the breath of My life into them.
The DNA of my essence.
My complete person.
All that I have to impart,
You were given to cover the nations.

A Love that is full and complete in Me.
No one can change what I put into you.
No one can claim that it was otherwise.
I will manifest myself in you for all to see.

You had no other training except by Me.

You are formed and molded by Me.

My hand scooped out the areas that were not of Me.

Areas that were left undone, My Mighty hand formed your heart to conform to mine.

Your heart looks like mine.

No malice, no rudeness, not hate, no impatience,

No vanity, no self-seeking, no evil,

No doubt or fear, not proud, not boastful,

Not destructive.

Your heart doesn't remember

When it has been wronged.

It is pure and has innocence.

My Mighty hand has kept you and protected you.

I have brought you into that place with Me

In perfect Love.

Your heart looks like mine.

This Fatherless generation is mine

And no one can have credit.

Man has abandon his relationship with Me.

So I have picked it up in My Great and Radical Grace and Mercy to bridge the gap,

The breach of My covenant with man.

I have produced a generation who will smell like Me, look like Me, taste like Me, act like Me,
Love like Me,
And show all the kindness to all people like I would.

There will be no mistake who My Fatherless are.
Because they are no longer Fatherless,
For I have not abandon them
Or left them by the wayside.

I have healed them,
Delivered them
And prepared them for the age ahead.

The New Day - The Reign of My Son.

So once again,
My ways of Love will be seen and felt.

Where man has abdicated his role with Me,
I have kept My word of My covenant
And picked up where man has laid down
His participation in My covenant.

I have raised up Sons and Daughters to reaffirm
My covenant and My Love for My people.

I have this Fatherless generation to be My brand,
My fiery brand on My Beloved.

They have gone thru more than anyone can bear.
They have suffered greatly for My names sake.
Their faith has brought them through.
The crushing they have endured
Has brought forth the fragrance of My Love.

My Love to be presented to the world.

The crushing wiped out all of themselves
And allowed Me to be fully present in them.

You will know them by their Love for each other.
The fragrance of their Love will permeate the world.
They truly are the heart of their Father.
Their absent fathers, fathers who abandon them,
Hurt them, who mistreated them,
Who they never saw, who left them,
Who didn't affirm them,
Who tried to destroy
Their own flesh and blood,

Their fathers who did every evil thing to them
And did not succeed
In keeping them from their destiny.

This Fatherless generation has been born with
Tender hearts toward Me
That the enemy has tried to destroy.

The intimacy that is within them the enemy has tried to fill
With every sexual sin,
Tried to destroy any hope of knowing their identity, tried to destroy with all of
the death culture,
Fill their hearts with every kind of lie about who I am.

The lie of self-leading to narcissism.
Every lie regarding worship of Me.
Every man made part of idol worship.
Every place in a man's heart to be turned elsewhere.
I am coming to bring out all the lies especially about intimacy with Me.

I am raising up those who have overcome.
They will rule and reign with Me.
I will bring them soon to fruition to expose the chains and lies holding back
My Presence.
My Glorious Presence.
My Glory which will permeate the earth,

No longer will the physical and the flesh
Hold back My people.

I will uncover the shame covering up My Glory.
I am calling to those shredded hearts by the enemy
To become whole in My presence.

All the pain will lift and the restoration will begin.
My people's hearts will be restored to Me.
Then, there will be Fathers connected to Me.
I am stepping up the gap between
Myself and My people.
Those who have suffered greatly at the hands of the enemy will have much
restored to them.
Restored in such a way that they will be renowned.
They will also be trusted with My Kingdom.

For they know Me.
For those who have suffered at the hands of the enemy from sexual perversion
the call is great...

Your heart was called
To carry a large capacity of love to My people.
The enemy stepped in to fill it with the wrong information to subdue the
Kingdom

With a message of subjection to the FLESH.

You are credited with great ability to carry the Love of My SPIRIT.
Satan has unduly attacked you so as not to be able to produce the Love you were created to carry.

You are overcoming generations of strongholds
(lies that we believe.)
Satan has not succeeded.

For some of you I am finishing your healing and will expedite it in this season.
I will finish you in due season.
I have started the surgery.
It will soon finish so the healing can begin.

Your hearts will be ready to bring forth the Love designed to change the world.
Your hearts will know
Your hearts will know for sure
That it is Me working in you.
Not something superficial or half way.
It will be a permanent work in your heart
For some of you it will seem a little strange at first
But I will make all things clear and distinct.

This will be a defining moment
You will not be foggy anymore
It will come forth with clarity

The Love is designed to bring others
Thru the same darkness you once knew
Or experienced.

They will carry their Daddy's heart
His fury will be unopposed in the coming days
Great healings and restoration
Will come upon the people
Something they have never experienced before.

Their love will far surpass anything that has ever been seen or will ever be seen again.

For they will truly carry their Daddy's heart.

This generation will overcome the workings
Of the flesh and show the overcoming
In the Spirit shown with
HIS GREAT LOVE.

Chapter Four

The Mature Prophet

The Prophet's Assignment

After the forming process is complete as we saw in the prior chapter, the Prophet will be given an assignment and carry out the instructions given to him. An important thought here is depending on the need for a certain type of Prophet. This will dictate the length of the maturing process.

In the following passage, we see that the Prophet Jeremiah was concerned that he was too young:

The call of Jeremiah

Jeremiah 1:1-9

The Lord said to me, "I chose you before I gave you life, and before you were born I selected you to be a Prophet to the nations." I answered, "Sovereign Lord, I don't know how to speak; I am too young." But the Lord said to me, "Do not say that you are too young, but tell them everything I command you to say. Do not be afraid of them, for I will be with you to protect you." I, the Lord, has spoken!" Then the Lord reached out, and touched my lips, and said to me, "Listen I am giving you the words you must speak. Today I give you authority over nations and kingdoms to uproot and pulldown and to destroy and to overthrow, to build and to plant."

We see in the next verses thru the end of Jeremiah chapter one, that he is asked what he "sees." God was not only engaging his seer gift, he was giving instruction.

Visions and instruction
Jeremiah 1:10-19

The Lord asked me, "Jeremiah, what do you see?" I answered, "A branch of an almond tree." "You are right," the Lord said," and I am watching to see that my words come true." Then the Lord spoke to me again. "What else do you see?" he asked. I answered, "I see a pot boiling in the north, and it is about to tip over this way." He said to me." Destruction will boil over from the north on all who live in this land, because I am calling all the nations in the north to come. Their kings will set up their thrones at the gates of Jerusalem and around its walls and also around the other cities of Judah. I will punish my people because they have sinned; they have abandoned me, have offered sacrifices to other gods, and have made idols and worshipped them. Get ready, Jeremiah; go and tell them everything I command you to say. Do not be afraid of them now or I will make you even more afraid when you are with them. Listen, Jeremiah! Everyone in this land - the kings of Judah, the officials, the priests, and the people-will be against you. But today I am giving you the strength to resist them; you will be like a fortified city an iron pillar and a bronze wall. They will not defeat you, for I will be with you to protect you. I, the Lord, has spoken."

Jeremiah was also receiving on the job training by the seat of his pants. If you look at the verse where it says, "But I am giving you the strength to resist them" Jeremiah was being given instant power for the task at hand. So we see a pattern here of God's sovereignty about how he will equip us for the job.

There is a process of maturing and God's provision of equipping along the way.

I often have wondered if this is a way to surprise the enemy when God uses these kinds of methods beside him just filling the need of that situation.

He once told me he could raise a kingdom in one day if he needs to and tear it down the next day!

Jeremiah's Prophetic ministry extended over forty years. Called to proclaim God's judgment upon Judah, his task was extremely difficult and painful. His fellow townsmen threatened his life if he continued preaching in God's name:

Jeremiah 11:21 "The men of Anathoth wanted me killed, and they told me that they would kill me if I kept on proclaiming the Lord's message."

His proclamation of the destruction of the Temple, brought the priests and Prophets charging him with blasphemy, a crime which carried the death penalty. For having declared Jerusalem's destruction he was beaten and chained. **Jeremiah 19:40-20:6** He was scorned, denounced, considered a traitor and thrown in a cistern left to die.

Throughout his ordeal the Prophet was deeply conscious that his message was God's **(Jeremiah chapter 1 verse 7-9)** and that he was under compulsion to deliver it. **(Jeremiah chapter 20 verse 9)** His hope and trust were in God.

As shown in previous chapters, the Prophet's life is quite painful and always challenged. The training seems redundant at times and downright brutal. The focus becomes God and only God. That is the sole intent so that the Prophet couples with God to get the job done.

The Prophet Carrying God's Heart

God's care for Israel

The Lord told me to proclaim this message to everyone in Jerusalem:

"I remember how faithful you were when you were young, how you loved me when we were first married; you followed me through the desert, through a land that had not been planted. Israel, you belonged to me alone; you were my sacred possession. I sent suffering and disaster on everyone who hurt you. I, the Lord have spoken."

Listen to the Lord's message, you descendants of Jacob, you tribes of Israel.

The Lord says, "What accusation did your ancestors bring against me?" What made them turn away from me? They worshipped worthless idols and became worthless themselves. They did not care about me, even though I rescued them Egypt and led them through the wilderness: a land of deserts and sand pits, a dry and dangerous land where no one lives and no one will even travel. I brought them into a fertile land, to enjoy its harvests and its other good things. But instead they ruined my dry land; they defiled the country I had given them.

The above Scripture passage is from **Jeremiah chapter 2 verses 1-7**.

This passage is a perfect example of how the Lord pours his heart out to the Prophet about the condition of the people and their relationship with him. Often the Lord shared his heart and the Prophet carried the message to the people. His heart of overwhelming love was exhibited towards his people even though they were wandering away from him.

The Prophet is held in high regard by being trustworthy to carry the message and the plan of God. It is held in the Prophet's heart until the right time to convey it. God knows the Prophet will not use it to hurt people or for his or her own personal gain. It is a specific plan that is not of this world. It is all about the Kingdom of God and nothing else.

The Prophet can be God's mouth piece because they can carry the vision and release it.

I often find it interesting how the tide of public opinion says there is no such thing as an Old Testament Prophet when in fact a Prophet is a Prophet. The method of how God and the Prophet function together still hasn't changed. The need for a Prophet still hasn't changed. What is misunderstood is that the Prophet is released for certain jobs and time periods. As previously stated, a Prophet will never tell you they are a Prophet and they usually are unrecognizable by the general body of believers.

The mature Prophet is sent out to various locations and places to carry and release God's heart to the people. The message carried to the people is about repentance, restoration, salvation, deliverance and healing. He or she brings direction, builds up and equips his fellow believers.

He or she belongs to God not the local house of worship. So he or she is often misunderstood because they do not flow the same way the local house flows. He or she is coming with help for the body of believers. He or she often is given very deep revelation about the condition of the body of believers they are sent to help.

It is not uncommon for them to be viewed as an intruder or outsider due to their "difference."

Chapter Five

Attributes of the Office of the Prophet

True Need for the Office of the Prophet

The Office of the Prophet is highly misunderstood because of the true need for one and lack of understanding of the call. The previously mentioned reasons cloud much of what we know today. This misunderstanding sends the body of believers on a goose chase unaware of what is currently taking place spiritually.

In this chapter, the spiritual condition of the Prophet that falls into line with the actual job duties of the Prophet will be discussed as well as the True need for the Prophet and the evidence of the call.

In **Jeremiah Chapter** two God declares his relationship with Israel in **verses 1-3**.

The Lord told me to proclaim this message to everyone in Jerusalem. "I remember how faithful you were when you were young, how you loved me when we were first married; you followed me through the desert, through a land that had not been planted. Israel, you belonged to me alone; you were my sacred possession. I sent suffering and disaster on everyone who hurt you. I, the Lord has spoken."

This is a strong statement from the Lord to his people regarding their relationship.

His never ending love for his bride is never far from his heart. He is a lover continuing to woo his bride and tell her how he feels. He has made known to her that he remembers how he feels toward her. This is the tender heart of God towards a people he is madly in love with. He will do anything to take care of her and watch over her.

In chapters two and three of Jeremiah, God tells of Israel's unfaithfulness. God's heart is always to restore his people back to himself. His heart aches for his bride to come back and participate in the marriage covenant he has with them. He reminds her over and over of what has transpired between them in these next chapters in Jeremiah.

God does not leave any stone unturned in this presentation of their unfaithfulness and their refusal to worship God.

Here are some of those scriptures. Only a few are listed here, but I would like to encourage you to read the chapters in their entirety.

Jeremiah chapter 2:4-9

Listen to the Lord's message, you descendants of Jacob, you tribes of Israel. The Lord says: "What accusation did your ancestors bring against me? What made them turn away from me? They worshipped worthless idols and became worthless themselves. They did not care about me, even though I rescued them from Egypt and led them through the wilderness: a land of deserts and sand pits, a dry and dangerous land where no one lives and no one will even travel. I brought them into a fertile land, to enjoy its harvests and its other good things. But instead they ruined the land; they defiled the country I had given them. The priests did not ask, "Where is the l Lord?" My own priests did not know me; the Prophets spoke in the name of Baal and worshipped useless idols.

Now skipping ahead to verse 20, which highlights their blatant disobedience:

The Sovereign Lord says, "Israel long ago you rejected my authority; you refused to obey me and worship me. On every high hill and under every green tree you worshipped fertility gods."

In these verses we see that God himself is showing the need for the Prophet to speak on his behalf. God uses the Prophet to intervene in the wayward life of his wife the nations of Judah and Israel. God knows when he needs to speak to his people and therefore uses the Prophet to carry out the heart of God. He makes it very clear about how they deserted God and made their own way instead of following God. That action (going their own way) led them off the path God laid out for them. Because God loves his people, he calls us back into relationship with him. The Prophet is used for this purpose. Pointing the people back to God. It is the people's true need for God. They are completely wayward and struggle greatly with their flesh not wanting to be regenerated by the work of the Holy Spirit. Their carnal nature rules them to the extent that God has to point out to them what they do and have done against the living God.

In Jeremiah, chapter 5, the Prophet Jeremiah gives lengthy description of what the people's heart condition is toward the Lord. Starting in verse 12, the Lord announces to Jeremiah what he wants to say to the people and what posture they have taken towards the Lord. He then tells Jeremiah to tell them what is about to happen because they are disobedient and defiant.

Let's look at these verses together:

The Lord rejects Israel

Jeremiah chapter 5:12-19

The Lord's people have denied him and have said, "He won't really do anything. We won't have hard times; we won't have war or famine." They have said that the Prophets are nothing but windbags and that they have no message from the Lord. The Lord God Almighty said to me, "Jeremiah, because these people have said such things, I will make my words like fire in your mouth. The people will be like wood, and the fire will burn them up." People of Israel, the Lord is bringing a nation from far away to attack you. It is a strong and ancient nation, a nation whose language you do not know.

Their bowmen are mighty soldiers who kill without mercy. They will devour your crops and your food; they will kill your sons and your daughters. They will slaughter your flocks and your herds and destroy your vines and fig trees. The fortified cities in which you trust will be destroyed by their army. The Lord says, "Yet even in those days I will not completely destroy my people. When they ask why I did all these things, tell them Jeremiah that just as they turned away from me and served foreign gods in their own land, so they will serve strangers in a land that is not theirs."

I believe it would be safe to say that God was not only angry, he called the people on their stuff and let them know this is what will now happen. He is a good daddy that will correct his children's path when they wander off. He will also tell them what to correct so they can get back onto the correct path. At this point, he is telling them this is what will happen because he has called them to repentance previously.

Jeremiah chapter 4:1-4

He warns and warns and then he has to take action. He is a righteous God. He loves his children. He also has to stay true to his nature. Therefore he continues going forward by taking action. The Prophet conveys this to the people and eventually God will act accordingly to the people's response to God. The Prophet is the go between or mediator before God. The Prophet understands the people's frailties but is obedient to God.

The true need for the Office of the Prophet is the fact that God has groomed and raised up this person to speak on his behalf to a wayward people who are the apple of his eye and he is madly in love with. He has sent his son to die for them and will not let them go to be taken over by the enemy. God has done everything for them including correcting their path which they have wandered from.

The evidence of the Call of a Prophet

The first evidence of the Prophet being called is that they will never point the people away from God's already laid out foundations.

They will never compromise in this area or any other area. This is and the following evidences are the outward manifestation of the call. There is a great demand on the Prophet's life for this call. To make it clear, their life is not their own. The outside world is often criticizing what they are doing, how they are living their lives and all that's involved. The demand is so great they are often considered an outcast, a loser, misinformed, lost from the mainstream, never listened to, discarded and most often abused in every area of their life by other people. People are guilty of trying to buy the free gift of God's presence and power that the Prophet walks in many times (for their own gain) and abuse their meek state.

They are avoided at all costs by most people. This is often where they are blocked to gain things in life that are basic needs for them. While they are learning about love, God's true love, they often have those around who withhold love (care) from them. It's is the heartache of every Prophet.

The Prophet has considered the cost because it is very great. They have been through the traumas of life that even one of those life events would destroy most people. If they are to have the heart of God (which will be detailed in the next chapter) they most certainly have been crushed, pressed, and everything that brings death to self. They will look like God and carry God's heart in the end. This is what God wants formed in the Prophet's heart to carry out God's will on the earth for the people and the kingdom of God.

True Love

The very things the Prophet has to endure and experience is what can be used to minister to the people with. This is what qualifies them. Tremendous suffering. They are completely healed and filled up with the power and love of God. Their lives have not been in vain. The perfume they carry is True Love.

To expand the understanding and bring forth the evidence of the Prophet pointing the people to the ways of God we need to define the word religion. This is the cited definition from Dictionary.com.

Word origin and history for the word religion as follows:

Circa1200, state of life bound by monastic vows, also "conduct indicating a belief in a divine power," from Anglo-French *religiun* (11c), Old French religion "piety, devotion; religious community", and directly from Latin religionem (nominative religio) "respect for what is sacred, reverence for the gods; conscientiousness, sense of right, moral obligation; fear of the gods; divine service, religious observance; a religion, a faith, a mode of worship, cult; sanctity, holiness" in Late Latin "monastic life" (5c.).

According to Cicero derived from *relegere* "go through again" in reading or in thought), from re- "again" (see re-) + legere "read". However popular etymology among the later ancients (Servius, Lactantius, Augustine) and the interpretation of many modern writers connects it with *religare* "to bind fast" via the notion of place an obligation on, or "bond between humans and gods." In that case, the "re"-would be intensive.

Another possible origin is *religiens* "careful," opposite of *neligens*. In English, meaning "particular system of faith" is recorded from c. 1300; sense of "recognition of and allegiance in manner of life (perceived as justly due) to a higher, unseen power or powers" is from 1530s.

Here are some definitions of the word religion:

1. a. The belief in and reverence for a supernatural power or powers, regarded as creating and governing the universe: respect for religion.
b. A particular variety of such belief, especially when organized into a system of doctrine and practice: the world's many religions.
c. A set of beliefs, values and practices based on the teachings of a spiritual leader.
2. The life or condition of a person in a religious order: a widow who went into religion and became a nun.
3. A cause, principle or activity pursued with zeal or conscientious devotion: a person for whom art became a religion.
Idiom: get religion-Informal
1. To become religious or devout.
2. To resolve to end one's immoral behavior.

The word religion is undeniably a man-made definition. It never once refers to The Bible origin. The above mentioned definition and etymology are not pointing to a covenant relationship with the living God of The Bible. It is an attempt to bring the God of the universe down to our level of thinking.

The word religion only exists in the New Testament, in the Greek language only five times and with different meanings. There is no word for religion in the Hebrew or the Aramaic text in the Old Testament.

According to the Strong's concordance the word religion is contained in the following verses:

Acts 26:5, Galatians 1:13, 14, James 1:26, 27

The two Greek words are threskia (G2356) and loudaismos (G2454). The word threskia is defined as follows:

Fearing or worshipping God, trembling, to tremble or fearful.

The word *loudaismos* is defined as follows:

The Jewish faith and worship, religion of the Jews, Judaism.

The reason I chose this word to define is because it is a perfect example of our human thinking about how the kingdom of God works and is perceived.

The Prophet makes sure the ways of God are properly represented to the body of believers and pointed in the right direction. The Prophet usually is looked upon as going a different direction than the mainstream body of believers but in actuality that's how far off the body has travelled.

The Prophet's evidenced call looks almost opposite at times of the mainstream body of believers. This is how you know there is a true need for the Office of the Prophet.

The people are very wayward off the path. God will not let the people get so far off the path that there is no way out or back. He will come pull us out of the mire and quicksand where we get stuck.

Chapter Six

The Prophet's spiritual condition

The Character of a Prophet

7 he Prophet's character represented *Yeshua*. *Yeshua* was Prophet, Priest and King.

These are the three offices *Yeshua* held. Their purpose and function is to build the Kingdom with God.

The Prophet reveals God's will to the people, speaks for God, and communicates truths that the people need to know. *Yeshua* did this when he came to do the will of the Father **(Luke 22:42)**, to reveal the Father **(Matt.11:27)** and to speak the things of the Father, **(John 8:28, John 12:49)**.

The Priest offered the sacrifice for sin to God. **(Ezekiel 44:27)** Then in the renewed covenant, Yeshua the High Priest was the sacrifice for sin. **(Ephesians 5:2, Hebrews 9:26-27; 10:12)** The Prophet suffers for the Kingdom. **James 5:10, Acts 7:52, Matthew5:12**

The King rules over a Kingdom. *Yeshua* was the King of the Jews. **(Matthew 2:2.)** In Matthew 27:11 *Yeshua* acknowledges he is the King of the Jews. King David is the prime example of a King who was also a Prophet. **(2 Samuel 5:3 and Acts 2:30)**

In light of all of the painful training the Prophet endures, the outward character is unmistakable. It will be fully evident in his or her life. The aroma of the fruit will increase as time goes on. Developed with the understanding that they will fully represent *Yeshua*. Often God has to hide the Prophet wherever they are located. They will have the imprint, authority and stature of the lawgiver to build the Kingdom.

The Prophet's attributes will be seen as follows:

1. The Apostle Paul was speaking of how the Apostles and the Prophets were taught by the Spirit of God, they develop inner strength that was rooted and grounded in love. It is for the purpose of God's Glory. **(Ephesians 3:13-21.)**

2. The Fruit of the Spirit shows the Prophet's flesh has been submitted to God and regenerated by the Holy Spirit. **(Ephesians chapter 5)**

3. Humility is a natural byproduct of the Spirit, man operating within the Prophet. **(Numbers 12:3, Matthew 21:5)**

4. The Prophet cannot be moved outside of God's will for the Kingdom and the people.

In **Exodus chapter 5**, Moses is faced with Pharaoh making the people's life tortuous because of the request to let the people go. Moses cannot cave in to the fact of more suffering brought onto the people.

Moses has to continue with the instructions God gave him.

5. The Prophet's lifestyle is not contrary to the true ways of God. The Prophet does not participate in pagan rituals. **(Deuteronomy chapter 13)**

6. The Prophet operates in an extremely high level of faith. The Prophet is fearless. **(1Kings 22:10-51)**

7. The Prophet is not a seeker of fame or to be known **(John 7:1-6)**

8. The love of God dwells in the Prophet. **(John 13:34, 35.)**

9. The major role of the Prophet is to intercede before the throne of God. **(1 Samuel 7:8)**

10. The Prophet pointed the people towards being separate from the world. Holiness, not profane. God wanted his people brought out of the world system, the country of Egypt (which means constriction and limit) to have his people separate and distinct. (Holy) **(1Peter 1:14-16, Exodus 8:20-23)**

These attributes are the core of the Prophet. There is much more, but only the basics are presented here in this book. The Prophet can be a complex subject and needs to be simplified.

Chapter Seven

The Role of the Office of the Prophet

The Duties of the Prophet

The responsibilities of the Prophet are varied and line up with their attributes. The Prophet is true to his or her nature and comes out in their response to God's heart for the people. The Prophet is the conduit for God to the people.

Here is a list of the Prophet's job duties with a brief description:

1. THE PROPHET SPEAKS

The Prophet speaks God's heart to the people. It can range from instruction to judgement. *Exodus chapter 3*

2. THE PROPHET INTERCEDES

The Prophet intercedes for the people. *1 Samuel 7-8.*

3. THE PROPHET IS INVOLVED

The Prophet is always involved in social justice. *Isaiah chapter 58:1-7, Amos chapter 2:6-8, Amos chapter 5 10, 12.*

4. THE PROPHET GUIDES

The Prophet points the people back to true worship from idol worship. *Jeremiah 10:1-10*

5. THE PROPHET WATCHES

The Prophet is a watchman. *Ezekiel chapter 3:16-27, Isaiah chapter 62:6*

6. THE PROPHET TEACHES

Prophets are teachers. *Ezra chapter 7:1-21, Nehemiah chapter 8:1-18.*

7. THE PROPHET WORSHIPS

Prophets are worshippers. *Psalm 15, 2 Samuel 12:20, 1 Chronicles 29:20.*

8. THE PROPHET DIRECTS

Prophets know the sign of the times to direct the people. *1 Chronicles 12:32.*

9. THE PROPHET OBEYS

Prophets must have total obedience. *1 Kings 13* According to this, disobedience will cost the Prophet.

10. THE PROPHET SEES

Prophets are seers and visionaries. *Jeremiah chapter 1:11-13.*

There are many more roles that the Prophet can be groomed for. These are just general categories.

The Prophets are created for very detailed tasks and sent to different people groups (nations).

God seasons the Prophet accordingly.

Chapter Eight

Authority

The Walk of the Prophet

7 he Prophet carries a great deal of authority in the Kingdom. The authority is what determines the Prophet walking in an Office. The authority is gained by God's guidance and the Prophet's obedience to His word.

This is what determines a true Prophet from a false Prophet. Is the Prophet obedient to the will and leading of God? The throne of God is based on authority and authoritative values. God's throne is based on authority and the works of God come out of that.

A false Prophet walks in legalism and self-righteousness. **Romans verse 10:2-3.** They are disobedient. The disobedience looks like a whitewashing and bending of the truth. They make up their own rules and twist what God has told them to do. They abuse their authority and usually it's for their own gain in some way. **Numbers chapter 22.**

The true government of God is based on His laws, which represent His authority. He created the universe and all is upheld by His authority. All authority is appointed by God.

If we are to serve God, as the Prophet does, we must know his authority.

The following scriptures are valuable to read on this subject:

Hebrews 1:3, Isaiah 14:12-14, Matthew 6:13; 26:62-64.

Rebellion against God's authority is a violation of God's holiness. **Ezekiel chapter 28**

Lucifer rebelled against God's authority and this resulted in him getting kicked out of heaven. **Isaiah 14:1-23.** It is a classic example of what happens when you come against the authority of God.

Let us look at the definition of authority:

Authority-The power to enforce laws, exact obedience, command, determine, or judge.

www.thefreedictionary.com

It is safe to say that the foundation of God's government are His laws based on His authority.

Next look at the Hebrew definition for the word authority. It is Strong's word **H8630**.

The translation is *taqaph*. It is a primitive root word. It is translated to prevail over or against, overcome, overpower.

The Greek word is *exesti*. Strong's **G1832**. It is translated, as it is lawful. God's authority reigns. It is the basis of who He is. When we migrate from this we now have taken the glory from God.

So when we pray to Our Father, we are saying bring your laws and your authority to rule and reign on the earth. God's desire is to establish His authority on the earth. One of the things He uses is Prophets to co-labor with him to establish the Kingdom thru submission (obedience) to Him.

The Prophet can only gain the authority he needs to do the job by submitting to authority. The authority is God and His ways. So the Prophet then has permission to establish the Kingdom here on the earth. He has the authority. God trusts the Prophet.

Through *Yeshua*'s obedience to the Father by dying on the cross he afforded all of mankind grace for salvation. **(Hebrews 1, Romans 1:5, Philippians 2:8, 1 Corinthians 15:3, Romans 5:19)** If he had not suffered and died he would not have made the way for us to have everlasting life. He was submitted and obedient to God to do what the Father asked to pay the price for our redemption.

Obedience and submission brings humility. It is death to self. It is the loss of the false identity we are born with and provides our true identity in *Yeshua*. We have the correct information then to rule and reign with Him. We are prepared to operate in the Kingdom with Him. Think of it like going to school to be a brain surgeon. We have many years of school to prepare to do the job. We obtain the correct information to be that brain surgeon. If we did not submit to the process we would never be able to participate. The submission to a school requires us to put down our own thinking in order to perform brain surgery, otherwise we would never get the job. **(Hebrews 5:8, 1Peter 1:14, Romans 6:16, Titus 3:1, Romans 1:5)** Humility says "I will put down my own thinking to accomplish your will God." I will not be insistent to do it my way, my thinking. It says, "I am willing to obey what you want me to do and how to do it." This is how the Kingdom is established. God's wisdom is that we are the vessels submitted to Him and all will be accomplished in our obedience in what He tells us to do. There is no other way. **(Luke 17:33)** God's ways are not our ways. In His infinite wisdom when we are obedient He orchestrates a behind the scenes wisdom that accomplishes more than we can ever know. **Isaiah 55:8, Matthew 6:33**.

Obedience is better than sacrifice. The sacrifice can still bring in self. Let's look at the scripture reference.

And Samuel said, "Has the Lord as great delight in burnt offerings and sacrifices, as in obeying the voice of the Lord? Behold, to obey is better than sacrifice, and to listen than the fat of rams. For rebellion is as the sin of divination, and presumption is as iniquity and idolatry. Because you have rejected the word of the Lord, He has rejected you from being king." Saul said to Samuel, "I have sinned, for I have transgressed the commandment of the Lord and your words, because I feared the people and obeyed their voice." **1 Samuel 15:22-24**

The process of gaining authority, is steeped in these above mentioned principles. Without this process the Prophet cannot walk into the Office they are called into. If they are going to carry out the ways of God to establish the Kingdom they have gone through this process.

Chapter Nine

Rebellion against Authority

The Prophet's Representation

7he rebellion against authority in the Kingdom of God goes back to the Garden where Adam and Eve fell into the lie or stronghold from Satan regarding their authority in the Garden. They had been instructed by God to abstain from a certain tree in the Garden. That tree was the tree of the knowledge of good and evil. God's intention was to spare them from the pain of the knowledge of these things. **Genesis 2:8**

The command is located in **Genesis 2:16-17**, revealing to Adam, the intent of God's heart about the instruction. Shortly after Eve was created out of Adam's rib the serpent was presenting Eve with the lie. We know that Adam would have instructed her to the command of God regarding the Garden. She was his help mate.

Eve repeated the exact command back to the serpent. **Genesis 2:2-3**. Then something interesting happens here. The serpent repeats back a twisted answer. The serpent did not repeat the command back. The serpent made her second guess what she just said. Remember she repeated the command back exactly. Here we go.

Genesis **3:4-5** but the serpent said to the woman, "You will not surely die. For God knows that when you eat of it your eyes will be opened, and you will be like God, knowing good and evil."

The serpent appealed to her FLESH. The serpent confused her by appealing to her flesh. He appealed to the mere fact that the fruit was a delight to her eyes and it would make her wise. He made her aware of her own pride. Until this point, Adam and Eve didn't even know they were naked and not ashamed. **Genesis 2:25.** The serpent was able to get Eve to take her eyes off of God and put them on herself.

He made her doubt the command of God. He twisted the truth.

The serpent presented her with a partial truth (legal loophole) to lead her away from God. Satan often gives us 95% truth and 5% lie to lead us where we do not belong. This is why it is so important to know our scripture. If we have distractions and things going on we will miss these kind of subtleties. Satan is always hoping we will miss the fine print.

The next passage **Genesis 3:6-24** tells us that God confronted Adam and Eve and they took no accountability for their behavior and they suffered the consequences of what they did. The action of the rebelling against the authority of God led to the following:

The Lord God said to the serpent, "Because you have done this, cursed are you above all livestock and above all the beasts of the field; on your belly you shall go, and dust you shall eat all the days of your life. I will put enmity between your offspring and her offspring; he shall bruise your head, and you shall bruise his heel."

To the woman he said, "I will surely multiply your pain in childbearing; in pain you shall bring forth children. Your desire will be for your husband, and he shall rule over you."

And to Adam he said, "Because you have listened to the voice of your wife and have eaten of the tree of which I commanded you, 'You shall not eat of it,' cursed is the ground because of you; in pain you shall eat of it all the days of your life; thorns and thistles it shall bring forth for you; and you shall eat the plants of the field. By the sweat of your face you shall eat bread, till you return to the ground, for out of it you were taken; for you are dust, and to dust you shall return."

The man called his wife's name Eve, because she was the mother of all living. And the Lord God made for Adam and for his wife garments of skins and clothed them. Then the Lord God said, "Behold, the man has become like one of us in knowing good and evil. Now, lest he reach out his hand and take also the tree of life and eat, and live forever-" therefore the Lord God sent him out from the garden of Eden to work the ground from which he was taken. He drove out the man, and at the east of the Garden of Eden he placed the cherubim and a flaming sword that turned every way to guard the way to the tree of life.

God directly addressed their disobedience and its consequences. They lost their position in the garden. More importantly, they lost their right standing with God. They now put themselves into a position of needing to be redeemed, instead of a son and daughter with authority with the King of the universe and His Kingdom.

A Prophet who represents the Kingdom of God walks in authority. He or she cannot be walking in non-submission or lawlessness. The Prophet has to be submitted to the foundation God himself laid. The opposite would be impossible for nothing would stand or be eternal. It would become temporal or not everlasting.

Submission to authority is the central theme of a relationship with God. Prophets are experts at this action toward God. It is in their DNA to trust God to go the way He has laid out for His Kingdom.

Submission is simple obedience. If we trust God and believe him obeying comes naturally. A child naturally trusts us if we are acting in a loving manner towards our children.

God is no different.

Chapter 10

The Heart of GOD

The Expression of the Prophet

In this *final* chapter, I would like to expound on the outward manifestation of the Prophet's identity and how it applies to the Prophet's expression.

The word of God is literally in us and it is *ALIVE*!

Hebrews 4:12, "For the word of God is living and active, sharper than any two edged sword (literally dual purpose) piercing to the division of the soul and the spirit, of joints and the marrow, and discerning the thoughts and intentions of the heart."

The Word **(John 1:1, John 1:14)** states that *Yeshua* already existed, he was the same as God and was with God. Then it states that He became flesh on earth and walked among us seeing His glory and that of the glory belonging to the Father.

By *Yeshua*'s death on the cross, it made it possible for us to have full access or complete freedom to the Most Holy Place.

Hebrews 10:19-21 "We have, then, my brothers, complete freedom to go into the Most Holy Place by means of death of *Yeshua*. He opened for us a new way, a living way, through the curtain-that is, through his own body. We have a great priest in charge of the house of God."

Then in **John chapter 17**, which is rather lengthy but important to read in its entirety:

"After *Yeshua* finished saying this, he looked up to heaven and said, "Father, the hour has come. Give glory to your son, so that the Son may give glory to you. For you gave him authority over all mankind, so that he might give eternal life to all those you gave him. And eternal life means to know you, the only true God, and to know Jesus Christ whom you sent. I have shown your glory on earth; I have finished the work you gave me to do. Father! Give me glory in your presence now, the same glory I had with you before the world was made. I have made you known to those you gave me out of the world. They belonged to you, and you gave them to me. They have obeyed your word, and now they know that everything you gave me comes from you. I gave them the message that you gave me, and they received it; they know that it is true that I came from you, and they believe that you sent me. I pray for them. I do not pray for the world but for those you gave me, for they belong to you. All I have is yours, and all you have is mine; and my glory is shown through them. And now I am coming to you, I am no longer in the world, but they are in the world. Holy Father! Keep them safe by the power of your name, the name you gave me, so that they may be one just as you and I are one. While I was with them, I kept them safe by the power of your name, the name you gave me. I protected them, and not one of them was lost except the man who was bound to be lost- so that the scripture might come true. And now I am coming to you, and I say these things in the world so that they might have my joy in their hearts in all its fullness. I gave them your message, and the world hated them, because they do not belong to the world, just as I do not belong to the world. I do not ask you to, but I do ask you to keep them safe from the Evil One. Just as I do not belong to the world they do not belong to the world. Dedicate them to yourself by the means of the truth; your word is truth. I sent them into the world, just as you sent me into the world. And for their sake I dedicate myself to you, in order that they too, may be truly dedicated to you. I pray not only for them, but also for those who believe in me because of their message. I pray that they all may be one. Father! May they be in us, just as you are in me and I am in you. May they be one, so that the world will believe that you sent me. I gave them the same glory you gave me, so that they may be one, just as you and I are one. I in them and you in me, so that they may be completely one, in order that the world know you sent me and that you love them as you love me. Father you have given them to me, and I want them to be with me where I am, so that they may see my glory, the glory you gave me; for you loved me before the world was made. Righteous Father! The world does not know you, but I know you, and these know that you sent me. I made you known to them, and I will continue to do so, in order that the love you have for me may be in them, and so that I also may be in them."

This is the perfect picture of *Yeshua* pleading with God the Father on our behalf for us to know the Father. Our Christian walk is much like this conversation *Yeshua* had with the Father. We want everyone to know God and how he loves us. We will shout it from the house tops to let everyone know.

It also shows the picture of the abiding and the identity *Yeshua* wants us to walk with. *Yeshua* states he wants for us exactly what the Father gave him. He then goes on to say it is for us and the world to know that the Father loves us and sent us into the world.

The heart of God is put into the Prophet to carry out the work of ministering to the people. Love is the central theme. The picture from **John chapter 17** is a good start of God's heart to be in us. I find it interesting that the glory is one of those things that *Yeshua* wants us to have. It is not unreachable or impossible. It is a priority.

The Love that the Prophet carries is rooted in obedience. In **John chapter 14 verse 15** it states, "If you love me you will keep my commandments."

The Prophet is obedient. He also Loves (cares) about what God wants. God's heart is for us to have life. **John chapter 14 verse 21**, "Whoever accepts my commandments and obeys them, is the one who loves me. My Father will love whoever loves me; and manifest myself to him."

The passage goes onto say that *Yeshua* will leave them with peace.

The word peace from the Hebrew root word **H7999** from the Strong's concordance means to be in a covenant of peace, be at peace, to be complete, to be finished, be ended, to make safe, whole or good or restore, make compensation, to make good, to be sound, to be uninjured, to requite, recompense, reward, to be repaid.

The Hebrew word for peace from the Strong's **H7965** goes on with the following:

Completeness, safety, soundness in body, welfare, health, prosperity, peace, quiet, tranquility, contentment, quiet, tranquility, contentment, friendship, of human relationships, with God especially in covenant relationship, peace from war.

I am using the Hebrew word for this because the Greek counterpart does not lend itself to depth of translation. It is not very descriptive. I often go to the Hebrew first because it gives a better picture.

The outcome of obedience is perfect peace. This is the very thing we avoid if we refuse to submit to the living God. His ways are better than our ways. We are able then to stand for God and not our flesh.

Flesh brings fear.

Conclusion

God's intention was to equip the Prophet in all areas of their life and to prepare them for the work God has for them. He especially wants them to carry His heart.

Yeshua made it possible to completely fulfill this by his death on the cross.

His example of obedience makes the way for the Prophet to build the Kingdom. He has authority due to his obedience. Joshua was sent into the land due to his obedience.

According to **Zechariah chapter 3:6-7 NIV,** The angel of the Lord gave this charge to Joshua. "This is what the Lord Almighty says: 'If you walk in obedience to me and keep my requirements, then you will govern my house and have charge of my courts, and I will give you a place among these standing here."

The fullness of the Prophet has to do with authority due to obedience. He or she then can carry out all the functions of the Kingdom.

The Office of the Prophet is needed today! We are in the midst of shaking and governmental alignment to the Kingdom of the living God. We are not just being aligned for a revival, this is truly for the Kingdom coming.

On earth as it is in heaven.

About the Author

Sharon Luzzi has resided in Rancho Cucamonga California since 1979. She raised and homeschooled three beautiful children – Allison, Kristen and Michael. Sharon also has two precious grandchildren – Jackson and Ella.

An ordained minister, Sharon is very active in her church. Her ministry includes children, crisis intervention, sound engineer and teacher.

Sharon is also concerned with her community and has been involved in such events as Pro-Life, National Day or Prayer, Prayer Breakfast, and the Inland Valley Republican Assembly where she was the Vice President for five years and served as co-chairman for the State CRA convention.

Sharon's favorite place to be is at the beach or anywhere outdoors. She loves photography, riding horses, animals, exotic cars, writing worship songs and learning more about her art skills.

References

Dictionary.com

Blue Letter Bible

Bible versions used: NASB, ESV and St Jerome

Contact The Butterfly Typeface Publishing For all your Publishing & writing needs!

Iris M Williams
PO Box 56193
Little Rock AR 72215
501-681-0080

www.butterflytypeface.com